LITTI
CURRY

THE LITTLE BOOK OF CURRY

Text by Stephanie Buick

An Hachette UK Company
www.hachette.co.uk

Summersdale Publishers Ltd
Part of Octopus Publishing Group Limited
Carmelite House
50 Victoria Embankment
LONDON
EC4Y 0DZ
UK

www.summersdale.com

Printed and bound in the UK

ISBN: 978-1-80007-417-0

Substantial discounts on bulk quantities of Summersdale books are available to corporations, professional associations and other organizations. For details contact general enquiries: telephone: +44 (0) 1243 771107 or email: enquiries@summersdale.com.

The
LITTLE BOOK OF
CURRY

Rufus Cavendish

Contents

Introduction

In the low-slung plains between the deserts of Rajasthan and the foothills of the Himalayas lies the excavation site of Farmana. Here, in northern India, archaeologists have unearthed fire-scorched clay pots containing traces of aubergine, turmeric, garlic and ginger. These 4,000-year-old vessels might well have contained some of the earliest curries ever made. The human desire to bring excitement to ordinary ingredients by fusing them with spices is, it seems, truly ancient and abiding. Whether we crave it for its lip-tingling heat, mouth-watering aromas, perky pulses or tender, slow-cooked meat, curry has evolved over millennia to become arguably the world's most popular dish.

The story of curry is long and convoluted, involving ancient medicine, a Hindu god, invaders and colonizers, migration, enterprising merchants, bloody sea battles and perilous treks along the Silk Road. Your own curry journey has probably been far less eventful. In the absence of high drama, you may well have enjoyed in relative peace some belt-loosening dishes of beefed-up rendang, indulgent korma or eye-watering vindaloo.

But the hope of this book is that, the more you know about curry – where it came from, how it's made and why it became so globally successful – the more you'll appreciate it as you take your seat at the table or head into the kitchen to make one yourself.

Over the coming pages, we'll look at the differences among various curries and at the key spices and ingredients that are used to produce those fantastic flavours. We'll briefly explore the colourful history of curry and the people who took it all over the world. We'll take a look at the origins and characteristics of some of the most well-known curries. And finally, we'll round off our journey with some tasty recipes, as you'll no doubt have worked up a healthy appetite.

THE WONDERFUL WORLD OF CURRY

From the sumptuous, regal cuisine of northern India to the bright, fiery curries of tropical South East Asia and the earthy, hot-hot-hot dishes of the Caribbean, curry is now truly global and the options and variations available are as diverse as the people who cook them. But curry had to start somewhere before it got everywhere.

In this FAQs chapter, we will explore the origin of curry and the historical influence of invaders and settlers on Indian cuisine, debunking a few myths along the way. We will also see how curry was taken all over the world and evolved into the universally loved, very distinctive dishes we know today.

What is curry?

Although definitions and cooking methods vary, let's say that a curry is any dish containing meat, fish, pulses or vegetables with a spiced sauce. It is usually accompanied by a starch-based food such as rice, naan bread, chapatis or dosa pancakes.

It's thought the word "curry" comes from the South Indian state of Tamil Nadu, when in the early 1500s Portuguese rulers developed a taste for the spicy sauces that were made by local people. These sauces, they were told, were called *kari* or possibly *carree*. The Portuguese adopted the word and it changed to *curry*. Over time, particularly among the British, it has become a generic term for any Indian dish which contains a spiced sauce. The sauce is often referred to as "gravy", which is another legacy of British rule in India.

There is no doubt that "curry" originated in India, but the clearly defined array of dishes we know today, with instantly recognizable names such as rogan josh, korma or vindaloo, have never been referred to by Indians as curry.

How many kinds of curry are there?

There is no agreed means of curry classification, but we can certainly see some clear differences between the different types of curry enjoyed around the world. The easiest distinction is between the simple and the complex. The former tend to be everyday curries containing humble ingredients like dhal (lentils) or aloo gobi (potatoes and cauliflower). These may be served as a side dish to a larger helping of curry, or quickly prepared as a street food and eaten with dosa pancakes or roti (a thin flatbread).

Complex curries tend to contain a greater mix of ingredients and involve a longer cooking process. They are typically prepared for celebrations and special occasions – for example, the great dishes of biryani which are proudly served at wedding banquets, often decorated with silver leaf.

Another basic difference is between dry and wet curries. A dry curry, such as a bhuna or rendang, contains very little gravy, often because it's been cooked for a long time to reduce the liquid, resulting in an intense concentration of spices. Alternatively, a curry may be dry simply because the intention is to let the main ingredients speak for themselves rather than drowning them in sauce. Jalfrezi, which was influenced by Chinese stir-fry methods, is an example of this.

Wet curries, on the other hand, contain more gravy, sometimes enough to yield a soup-like consistency, such as the coconut milk-based curries of Thailand. Other wet curries may be thick and stew-like – for example, those from Japan, West Africa and the Caribbean.

Further distinctions may be made between heat and flavour profiles. For example, Japanese curries normally have little heat and tend to be savoury with a dash of sweetness. The gently spiced kormas and pasandas of northern India contain very little heat, with the emphasis on rich ingredients, such as flaked almonds and cream. The sour, eye-watering vindaloos of southern India are a very different beast, however, as are the searingly hot, coconut-rich curries of South East Asia and the earthy, blow-your-socks-off curries of the Caribbean.

Why do we love curry so much?

Most people will say they "love a good curry" and there's clearly something deeply satisfying about the variety of spicy dishes out there, but what is the secret to curry's success? In 2015, this question prompted a team of scientists in Delhi to analyse curry to find out why it is so universally loved.

After studying over 2,000 recipes, they found that chefs tended to blend, within any one particular dish, spices and other flavourings that had no chemical similarities. Durban curries are a good example of this: fiery cayenne and chilli contrast with sweet spices such as cinnamon and fennel. The result is a vibrant profusion of flavours.

In traditional Western cooking, chefs tend to pair similar flavours – for example, cheese and pasta, or beef and gravy. Tasty though they may be, the flavours overlap, so there is no interaction between them. You could think of it as the Western flavours holding hands and getting along nicely, whereas the curry flavours are also holding hands and getting along nicely while dancing their socks off.

How did curry begin?

The diverse cuisine of the Indian subcontinent is the result of thousands of years of influence from trade, exploration, invaders and colonizers. Over the ages, for example, Indian merchants exported spices such as pepper and cardamom to the Roman Empire, Central Asia, China and South East Asia, while merchants from these places introduced new spices to India in turn. Curry has always been about this cultural give and take, voluntary or otherwise.

The earliest origins of curry can be traced back to the ancient Indian teachings of Ayurveda, said to have come from Dhanvantari, the Hindu god of medicine, who is said to have emerged from an ocean of milk bearing ambrosia, the nectar of eternal life.

Ayurvedic principles emphasize the importance of balancing the foods in one's diet to keep the mind, body and spirit in harmony. There are six taste groups: sour, salty and spicy foods are considered to warm the body, whereas sweet, astringent and bitter foods are cooling. These principles of combining flavour profiles lay the groundwork for Indian cuisine. For example, the heat of chilli is cooled by fruits and yoghurt, and the combination of sourness and salt give lime pickle its bite.

The first curry ever made?

The ancient traces of food found in Farmana, in northern India, were of a simple aubergine curry. Here is a reconstruction of that curry with a little culinary artistic licence.

The dish serves 2 people.

INGREDIENTS

4 aubergines, chopped into large chunks

100 g red lentils

2–3 tbsp raw mango, cubed

4 cloves of garlic

2 tsp ginger

2 tsp fresh turmeric

½ tsp cumin seeds

½ tsp ground black pepper

3–4 tbsp vegetable oil

Salt and sugar (if needed) to taste

Roughly crush the cumin seeds (the back of a wooden spoon will do). Boil the lentils until half-cooked. Drain and set aside. Drop the aubergines into hot oil and fry on a high heat for a minute. Reduce the heat and add the rest of the ingredients. Simmer until the lentils and aubergine are fully cooked. Serve with unleavened bread, such as naan.

How did curry evolve in India?

THE PORTUGUESE

At the end of the 1400s and into the 1500s, the Portuguese established ports and trading posts along the palm-fringed shores of southern India. In search of cardamom, cloves and precious black peppercorns, they themselves brought tomatoes, potatoes, guava, corn and chillies, all booty from South America, together with salt-encrusted barrels of meat preserved in vinegar.

The Portuguese men integrated well, marrying local women and adopting the cuisine. In turn, the foods they had introduced had a profound influence on southern Indian cooking. Tomatoes and toddy vinegar (fermented palm wine) were also assimilated into local cuisine, proving to be just as effective souring agents as the indigenous tamarind and mango.

Previously, the Indians had used ginger and black peppercorns to add heat to food. However, as the Portuguese were now exporting so much black pepper out of India, the chilli became an ideal substitute. It flourished in the hot climate, its fame spread, it was embraced wholeheartedly by Indian cooks and nowadays curry is synonymous with chilli.

THE MUGHALS

In the 1520s, after successive waves of invasions, Babur the Tiger, the powerful Mughal emperor from what is now Uzbekistan, took control of northern India. The Mughals' cuisine differed beyond all recognition from the simple pots of meat and rice and skewered lamb cooked by Central Asian shepherds over open fires. The Mughals adored food and their frequent palace banquets featured such heady delights as meat tenderized with spiced yoghurt then slow-cooked with layers of rice and sauce. They introduced to northern India new and exotic ingredients like saffron, rose water, almonds, pistachios, dried plums and raisins.

This all created a startling contrast between the Mughals, with their deep appreciation of a full stomach, and the Indians, who ate modest portions according to the principles of a balanced and healthy diet. With time, the dairy and meat-rich Mughal cuisine became assimilated into northern Indian cooking. The Indians, in turn, began to adapt Mughal cooking to suit their own tastes and introduced their own spices to the cooking pot.

THE BRITISH

When the British East India Company was formed at the beginning of the seventeenth century, it brought an influx of British personnel into India. Although the British were keen on Indian cuisine, and very good at adapting recipes to suit their own tastes, they did not have a great deal of influence on Indian cuisine, unlike the Mughals and Portuguese. The British retained their relatively delicate palate and became fond of the rich, meat-based Mughlai dishes which, although spicy, were not too hot.

Their Indian cooks turned down the heat accordingly, and as the years went by, anglicized versions of Indian recipes began to emerge from the kitchens of the Raj. Khichri, for example, which was a Mughlai dish of lentils and rice, lost its lentils, acquired smoked fish and boiled eggs and became kedgeree, a popular breakfast among British families. Similarly, mulligatawny, a mildly spiced meat soup, evolved from rasam, the tamarind-based southern Indian soup.

THE EVOLUTION OF CURRY POWDER

Curry powder, a pre-prepared mixture of spices, has a story of its own to tell. Usually bright yellow, it's seen by many as a handy shortcut in the curry-making process, but it is eschewed by purists who insist that the only authentic way to prepare a curry is to select and grind the spices yourself. Certainly, it was never used in traditional Indian cooking. Whichever view you take, there is no denying it is the quickest and most convenient way to prepare a curry.

In commercial terms, pre-blending the spices made it cheaper than transporting them all individually. The first known advertisement for curry powder appeared in 1784, and the ingredient grew in popularity during the early-to-mid 1800s as various different blends – such as Madras, Bengal and Delhi – became available.

By the mid-to-late 1800s, British companies were selling ready-made curry powders and pastes. Hot, spicy food, they claimed, would stimulate the blood circulation, resulting in a healthy digestion and a vigorous mind.

These claims were eagerly accepted by many and those who could afford it were soon using these products to jazz up their curries. The austere Victorians also believed in thrift, so the use of a ready-made powder became a quick way for wealthy families to use up their scraps of leftover meat in a curry.

In Australia, around the same time, curry powder became a significant import, with the leading brand being developed in Tasmania. Recipes for curry in the nineteenth century suggested using it with tomato soup, sultanas, bananas and even jam.

Elsewhere, in the Caribbean, it's likely that curry powder evolved as a result of the spices available locally when indentured workers settled there. Containing allspice and thyme, Jamaican curry powder is unique. Its higher than usual turmeric content also gives the curry an earthy taste, while the significant amounts of Scotch bonnet chilli make it very hot.

Overall, despite its rejection by curry foodies, this ubiquitous powder remains popular and is still finding its way into "non-curry" dishes – coronation chicken, devilled eggs and German currywurst being just a few examples.

How did curry become a global dish?

We have seen how two very distinctive culinary styles emerged on the Indian subcontinent: rich, meat-heavy cuisine in the north and, by contrast, lighter, fiery-hot fish and vegetable dishes in the tropical south. So how did curry then make its way around the world?

When people travel they take their food with them, and just as those people change and evolve when they travel, so does their cooking. No food is as well travelled and highly evolved as Indian cuisine.

Traders, indentured labourers and migrants all took recipes and ingredients to different corners of the world. As the generations passed, Indian cuisine evolved to the extent that many dishes today bear little or no resemblance to those left behind all those years ago. Others, however, remain exactly the same. For instance, the searing heat many of us associate with vindaloo is nothing like the perky sourness of the original pork dish of southern India. On the other hand, the Mauritian street food of roti (flatbread) filled with dhal and pickles has changed very little.

THE BRITISH TOOK CURRY HOME

During the 1700s, spicy food had largely gone out of favour in Britain due to a prevailing belief that it heated the blood and inflamed the libido. Not wishing to overexcite their carnal appetites, the British reserved spices such as nutmeg, cloves and cinnamon for desserts and baking, but for main courses they dutifully stuck to dishes like stew, roast meats and fish pie with plain vegetables such as potatoes, cauliflower and beans.

However, culinary change was afoot. By Queen Victoria's reign during the 1800s, there was a growing fascination with Indian culture and exotica. Artefacts, paintings, trinkets and furniture were shipped to the UK by various routes, and Anglo-Indian cuisine also made the journey across the waves. British people living in India sent recipes to family and friends at home who would then try them out in their own kitchens, and when whole families returned, they often took their servants, children's nannies and cooks with them.

In 1887, Queen Victoria's servant, Abdul Karim, who later became her close friend, served her a curry. It wasn't the first time she'd had one, but it made a lasting impression because that night she wrote in her diary, "Had some excellent curry prepared by one of my Indian servants."

From then on she requested her kitchen staff to prepare curry on a regular basis, and thereby may have unwittingly fuelled the nation's growing interest in Indian cooking, as the rest of the country (or rather those who could afford it) often sought a certain cachet by following the eating habits of the royals.

To an Indian household, the mild, watery curries of Britain would have been unrecognizable and insipid. Meat was simmered in stock with onions and curry powder and perhaps a few coriander seeds and some ginger. Instead of tamarind or mango, local produce like apples or plums would be added to the cooking pot, followed by a dash of lemon juice or coconut. Anglicized curries began appearing in recipe books and the wealthy sectors of British society, now presumably unconcerned about inflaming their libidos, took to devouring pilau rice, curry and spicy chutneys.

SYLHET

During the mid-1800s, the town of Sylhet (known then as Bengal) was carved up by waterways and rivers and had become a busy port. Until the 1940s, lascars (Indian sailors) were recruited there to stoke the fires of steamships bound for the UK, but the working conditions were so dangerous that many jumped ship in London.

A community of Bengalis formed around the back streets near the East London docks. They took over many of the run-down fish-and-chip shops after the Second World War and by the 1960s, Indian restaurants with red flock wallpaper and exotic music had become popular in the capital.

Today there are over 80,000 curry houses in the UK, the majority of them run by Bangladeshis.

AUSTRALIA

Nearly all immigrants to Australia in the nineteenth century were from Britain. Curry became just as popular down under, and not dissimilar to the anglicized, stew-like curries being prepared in the UK.

For Australian immigrants, as with everywhere else, it was necessary to adapt to whatever was locally available, so pineapple, mango and coconut were used in their curries, together with imported spices such as coriander seeds, turmeric and ground ginger. Thus, curry became an effective way to turn unfamiliar ingredients such as wombat meat, iguana tails or the wattle bird into a hearty meal. Mrs Beeton's *Book of Household Management*, published in 1861, gives a recipe for "kangaroo tail, curried".

During the mid-twentieth century, in Australia as well as the UK, the culinary influence of migrants from Asian countries heralded a shift away from the generic, curry powder-based curries. New cookery books with Asian recipes became available and restaurants run by South Asian migrants offered Indian, Thai or Sri Lankan cuisine.

TRADING ROUTES

The curries of Malaysia and Indonesia are a good illustration of the way movement along trade routes leads to the fusion of ingredients and thus new styles of cuisine. When merchants from Tamil Nadu, in the south of India, and Gujarat, from the west, travelled to Malaysia and Indonesia in search of spices, they introduced southern Indian cooking and spices.

Here, in South East Asia, fruity herbs and spices such as lime leaves and lemongrass were commonly used, together with star anise – a warming, liquorice spice which had already been introduced by Chinese traders.

The Indians had taken red and green chillies with them, so the new curries received generous amounts of these to give them a blitz of heat. To bring balance, the fiery chillies were calmed by the creaminess of coconut milk. The result was a light, highly aromatic curry which went perfectly with the local fish and seafood. This very distinctive combination of flavour profiles spread throughout Malaysia and Indonesia and persist to this day, giving South East Asian curries their instantly recognizable aromas.

INDENTURED LABOURERS

By far the most common way curry travelled around the world was by means of indentured workers and servants. The abolition of slavery in the British Empire in the 1830s created a labour shortage, so over a period of 80 years 1.5 million Indians were recruited to work on numerous sugar, palm oil, tea and coffee plantations. They travelled to British Guiana (now Guyana), the Caribbean islands, South Africa, Malaysia, Sri Lanka, Mauritius and Fiji. Food rations were meagre, consisting of flour, dhal (lentils), rice and a little ghee (a kind of clarified butter) or oil, so a dhal roti became standard fare. Wages were minimal, so migrants needed to adapt their cooking according to the foodstuffs they could afford and the ingredients locally available.

Most indentured workers never returned to their native lands, and it is easy to see why maintaining a strong food culture would have enabled them to retain a sense of identity and connection to home.

THE WORLD'S BIGGEST CURRY

The largest curry ever cooked was made by a team of chefs from the Indian Chefs and Culinary Association in Singapore on 1 August 2015. Prepared in a public park at the annual Suvai Indian Gourmet Festival, the curry weighed 15.34 tonnes (33,838.9 lb) and needed an 11-metre cooking vessel.

The largest-ever naan bread was made on 19 April 2016 in Toronto, Canada, by Loblaw Companies Limited. At 4.96 m (16 ft, 3.24 in.) in length and weighing in at 32 kg (70 lb), it would have been a perfect match for the world's biggest curry.

SOUTH AFRICA

During the 1600s, the Dutch East India Company took slaves to South Africa. They came from a wide territory encompassing India, Malaysia and Indonesia and became collectively known as Cape Malays. A couple of hundred years later, hundreds of thousands of indentured Indians were brought in by the British. Traders and merchants followed and, over the years, two distinctive styles of curry evolved: Malay and Durban.

Malay curry commonly contains fruit, such as apricots and raisins, which give it a sweet and sour tang. Its mildness is due to the sweeter spices such as coriander, cardamom and cinnamon. It is served with that old favourite, roti, and is enjoyed all over South Africa.

Durban curry contains copious amounts of chilli and cayenne. It is rich and oily, with a high tomato content that gives it an acidic flavour profile and a deep red colour. It is Durban curry which is used for the fast-food dish known as bunny chow.

Bunny chow is well loved and ubiquitous throughout Durban. It consists of a loaf of bread, or *kota* (quarter loaf), hollowed out and stuffed with curry. One theory as to its origin is that Indians working in the sugar-cane plantations replaced their traditional dhal roti with the more robust bread loaf filled with dhal or bean curry. Wages for indentured workers were so meagre, however, it is unlikely they could have stretched to a daily loaf.

The most likely explanation is that it was created by the enterprising Gujaratis who opened cafes and takeaways during the 1940s. Indians were often known throughout the Indian Ocean as *Banyans*, derived from *bania,* a caste of merchants and moneylenders. In South Africa, they became known as "bunnies". Their curries became very popular among the indigenous population, but under apartheid rule it was illegal for Black people to eat at these cafes. The solution was bunny chow, discreetly sold at the back door.

MAURITIUS

Two-thirds of the population of Mauritius are of Indian origin and they have had a big impact on the evolution of Mauritian cuisine. Historically, indentured labourers here supplemented their rations of rice, dhal and ghee by growing their own vegetables and spices. Happily, garlic, chilli and turmeric already grew on the island, having been planted by Indian settlers the previous century.

Today, a standard Mauritian street food is *dalpuri,* a pancake made from split peas. It's usually stuffed with vegetables, butter-bean curry and achar (pickled vegetables) and splashed with a Creole sauce. Biryani is also eaten in Mauritius with the addition of tamarind.

The modern curries of Mauritius, the Seychelles and the Maldives usually feature fish as well as coconut milk and tamarind. These curries are intensely flavoured with fragrant spices such as coriander seeds, green cardamom, ginger, cinnamon and star anise to create dishes with a distinctly southern Indian feel.

FROM CURRY TO SOAP

The first Indian-run curry restaurant in the West was opened in Marylebone, London, in 1811 by Sake Dean Mahomed, a Bengali entrepreneur and former captain of the British East India Company. With Indian furnishings, hookah pipes and a menu featuring pilau rice, kedgeree and chutney, the Hindostanee Coffee House was designed to remind its customers of their time in the East.

Within two years, however, Dean Mahomed was bankrupt. Undeterred, he rolled up his sleeves, became a "shampooing surgeon" and opened a bath house in Brighton, where the exotic oils and "Indian medicated vapour bath" were a huge hit with the aristocracy, including the future King George IV.

THE CARIBBEAN

Most of the Indians who went to the Caribbean as indentured workers were from the mountainous region of Uttar Pradesh, in the far north of India, where curries are prepared with pre-roasted spices, making them rich and dark. These workers took with them okra, aubergines, plums, mangoes, jackfruit and tamarind – all common staples of Caribbean cooking today. Herbs such as curry leaves, mint and coriander were not available, so the stronger-tasting tropical plant shado (or chadon) beni was used instead. The Indian *sag* (spinach) curry was adapted by using instead the Jamaican callaloo, a similar vegetable. Europeans had already introduced certain herbs, including thyme, to the Caribbean and the new migrants began to put it in their curries. Thyme is now part of the landscape of Caribbean curries, but it would never be found in a curry anywhere else.

Chillies, which had become a regular feature in Indian cooking since the Portuguese had introduced them hundreds of years earlier, continued to be an essential ingredient, with the fiery Scotch bonnet becoming the chilli of choice, providing Caribbean curries with their intense heat.

JAPAN

From the late 1880s, Japanese people began to die of beriberi, a thiamine (vitamin B1) deficiency. When soldiers and sailors also succumbed to the condition, during the Russo-Japan war of the early 1900s, the Japanese navy compared their menus with those of the British navy. They realized their own fare was very high in white rice. The British, however, were feeding their sailors hearty beef curries thickened with flour. Both beef and flour are rich in thiamine, so an obvious solution for the Japanese was to put curry on the menu. The Japanese sailors' health improved and curry was then served to the soldiers where it was so eagerly received that the Japanese army even featured "meals of glamorous curry" in their advertising campaign.

During the twentieth century, curry became ever more popular in Japan and in the 1960s, a ready-made "curry roux" became available in the shops. This block of flour, fat and spices meant anyone could rustle up their own curry at home, and today the dish remains a regular meal in most Japanese homes.

FASCINATING
FLAVOURS

Whether slow-cooked, simmered or quickly fried, spices and aromatics are the vital ingredients that set curries apart from other cuisines. The magic happens when they fuse with the other ingredients to create irresistible aromas and often unexpected hits of flavour.

In this chapter, we will take a very brief look at the history of spices; you'll be introduced to some of the most popular ones and get advice on putting together a basic collection of spices, aromatics and herbs to enable you to start creating your own delicious curries. Once you're familiar with the characteristics of spices and how they transform during cooking, you'll soon be using them with confidence and skill. Finally, we'll look at some simple ways to grow your own at home.

Precious spices

Throughout history, the relentless demand for spices has sparked bloody battles, led mariners to cross treacherous oceans and enabled traders to become phenomenally rich. From the second century BCE, spices were transported with silks, porcelain, gold and silver by camel caravans back and forth from China to Europe along the Silk Road. These spices had a multitude of uses. Cumin, ginger and chilli were used as food preservatives, and black pepper, thought to be a cure for the bubonic plague, was transported from Asia to Europe, ironically taking the same journey along the Silk Road as the plague itself.

To Europeans, spices from far-flung places were fascinating and delicious and exotic – a symbol of wealth and power, so valuable that one stolen handful of black pepper was the equivalent of pulling off a major bank heist. However, the greatest appeal of spices has always been their ability to transform a pot of everyday ingredients into a vibrant and appetizing dish. They have been, and always will be, an essential and exciting ingredient of any curry.

Spice 101

Spices are the aromatic, non-leafy parts of a plant, such as the roots, bark, flowers, seeds or fruit. They are nearly always dried by the time they reach our kitchens and may be used whole or ground to a powder. Although their principal job is to infuse with flavour the main ingredients of a dish, they also introduce heat, texture and colour. Curry chefs all over the world use them differently to produce their own distinctive culinary styles. Knowing how to combine and layer spices is a skill which can take years to master, although you can have a lot of fun experimenting with their heady aromas along the way.

Spices may be involved in all stages of the curry-cooking process. They are mostly added at the beginning to give them time to combine with the main ingredients. They can also be added part-way though (garam masala, for example), while flavourings such as coconut or tamarind can be added at the end to provide the top notes.

Popular curry spices

🌿 **Allspice (pimento)** – A key ingredient in Caribbean curries, allspice is made from the dried berries of the Jamaican bayberry tree. You can make a substitute by blending 3½ tsp ground cinnamon, ½ tsp ground nutmeg and ¼ tsp ground cloves.

🌿 **Amchoor** – Made from powdered, dried green mangoes, amchoor will add a sweet yet tart zing to curry. It's also a key ingredient in chaat masala, a pungent spice mix sprinkled over street snacks and fruit.

🌿 **Black mustard seeds** – Drop these bitter seeds into hot oil and watch them dance as they unleash their bitter flavour.

🌿 **Black pepper** – If cardamom is the queen of spices, black pepper is the king. The bite of this dried berry, native to steamy Kerala in South India, was once so sought after it was used as currency, hence the term "peppercorn rent".

🌿 **Cardamom** – Highly prized since ancient times, green cardamom is known as the "queen of spices". The knobbly, perfumed seeds are used in curries, desserts and even drinks.

Cinnamon – These reddish brown quills of bark, sometimes found bobbing around in cups of mulled wine, may be ground to a fine, dry powder or added whole to curry for a warmth and woody sweetness.

Cloves – These oddly medicinal-smelling seeds have an astringent aroma once cooked. They are used in pilau rice and are particularly popular in Caribbean curries. They have painkilling properties, particularly for toothache.

Coriander seeds – Often used in pickling, these piquant seeds carry a sweet, almost perfumed note. In earlier times, they were thought to be an aphrodisiac. Robert Turner, a seventeenth-century physician, observed that, when consumed with wine, "it stimulates the animal passions".

Cumin – In earlier times, some people believed that cumin stopped chickens and lovers from wandering, so women would give their sweethearts loaves of cumin bread before they went to war. More realistically, it pairs well with mustard seed and you can use it to ground your curry with savoury notes.

Fenugreek – These golden, nutty seeds, which manage to taste slightly sweet and deeply pungent at the same time, add a savoury depth to curries. The leaves can also be chopped and added at the end of the cooking process.

Galangal – This is a member of the same family as ginger and turmeric, so it carries the same citrus taste but is sharper and more peppery. It's an important ingredient in Thai, Malaysian and Indonesian cooking. Not always easy to get hold of, so you can always double up the ginger.

Ginger – The gorgeous citrus aroma from this zesty rhizome releases a powerful heat in curry. In around 500 BCE, Confucius observed that ginger removes dampness and fever so he included it in his diet.

Hing (**asafoetida**) – This sticky resin smells so unappetizing that it has been nicknamed devil's dung. But don't let that put you off – once cooked, it produces a wonderful onion-garlic flavour.

Star anise – The prettiest of all, this seven-pointed star brings a warm, liquorice aroma to cooking and features often in South East Asian curries.

Tamarind – The hard brown pods of the tamarind tree are available in a compressed block or as a rich, dark paste which is much sharper. Tamarind introduces a perky tang to curries.

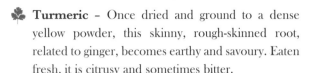 **Turmeric** – Once dried and ground to a dense yellow powder, this skinny, rough-skinned root, related to ginger, becomes earthy and savoury. Eaten fresh, it is citrusy and sometimes bitter.

GARAM MASALA

This versatile blend is often added towards the end of the cooking to generate a fragrant warmth. You can make it by blending the following:

1 tbsp ground cumin
2 tsp ground coriander
½ tsp ground nutmeg
1½ tsp ground black pepper
¼ tsp ground cloves
1 tsp cinnamon
1½ tsp ground cardamom
1 tsp chilli flakes (optional)

Starter spice collection

The range of spices used in curries can be mind-boggling, so here is a suggested collection of basic spices to get you started:

- Cumin
- Coriander seeds
- Cardamom
- Cloves
- Turmeric
- Cinnamon
- Chilli powder or flakes
- Fresh ginger and garlic

> For South East Asian curries, lemongrass, star anise, fresh coriander, lime leaves and coconut (creamed or canned) are essential basic ingredients. For Caribbean curries, allspice and fresh thyme.

Chillies

From mild jalapeños to the eye-watering Scotch bonnet, the choice of chillies is bewildering and it can be tricky to get the heat levels right. Too little chilli can fail to produce that gorgeous warmth we expect from a curry, but too much can turn your beautiful creation into an inedible horror.

As a rule of thumb, red chillies tend to be more fiery than green, and the smaller the chilli, the hotter it is. The flavour is in the main fruit while the seeds and white flesh contain most of the heat, so if you want to calm your chillies down, either cook them whole or slit lengthways and remove the seeds and flesh. You can also add a little sugar.

If you are unsure about cooking with chillies, the best way to get started is to buy one jar of chilli flakes or powder and familiarize yourself with using it. Most of the recipes later in this book assume medium-heat chilli flakes or powder, although a few do call for fresh chillies.

CHILLI HEAT LEVELS

Here is an illustration of how hot chillies can get. The numbers shown are each chilli's rating on the Scoville scale.

CAROLINA REAPER: 2,200,000

TRINIDAD MORUGA SCORPION: 2,009,231

GHOST PEPPER (BHUT JOLOKIA): 1,041,427

HABANERO: 577,000

SCOTCH BONNET: 325,000

BIRD'S EYE: 225,000

CAYENNE: 50,000

JALAPEÑO: 8,000

BELL PEPPER: 0

NUTMEG WARS

The Indonesian island of Rhun is a thickly forested, volcanic speck surrounded by treacherous sea. During the 1600s, it was one of the few places where nutmeg grew. This shiny brown nut was used to add warmth and sweetness to dhansaks (the Mughal dishes of northern India), Caribbean curries and the mild Anglo-Indian dishes which were popular at that time. The British, in pursuit of this precious spice, persuaded the indigenous population to hand over control in return for protection from the fearsome Dutch East India Company. After a long and bitter war, the Dutch took control of Rhun and in revenge the British seized the Dutch colony of New Amsterdam. After a four-year stalemate, both parties agreed they would each hold onto these territories. Hence, New Amsterdam became New York.

Herbs

🌿 **Coriander (cilantro)** – The chopped leaves of the coriander plant make a fantastic garnish for curries. The stalks are used in pastes for South East Asian curries.

🌿 **Curry leaves** – These elegantly formed leaves have a beautiful citrusy aroma and are commonly used in Sri Lankan and Malaysian curries. It's important to stick to fresh leaves, however, as they lose their flavour once dried.

🌿 **Lime leaves** – These bright, glossy leaves bring an uplifting, fruity top note to South East Asian curries.

🌿 **Mint** – This offers a cooling contrast to the heat of curry. Use it in the curry itself or finely shredded into yoghurt and cucumber raita (see page 115).

🌿 **Tej patta (Asian bay leaves)** – Much larger than the bay leaf, tej patta leaves have a mild cinnamon taste. If these aren't available, many cooks replace them with European bay leaves although the taste is very different and the jury's still out on whether their slightly minty aroma makes a good substitute.

SPICE MONSTERS

Medieval spice merchants were an unscrupulous but highly imaginative lot. To increase the value of their wares, they told tales of spices which only grew near swamps inhabited by writhing, poisonous snakes. Other spices were said to be found only on clifftops, guarded by enormous, hook-beaked birds.

Herodotus, the ancient Greek historian, wrote that cassia (a bark related to cinnamon) only grew in a lake infested by aggressive bat-like creatures which emitted terrifying screeches.

And just to make absolutely certain potential competitors were well and truly discouraged, the merchants embellished their stories with thrilling accounts of giant sea monsters lurking in the Arabian Sea.

Ways to prepare spices

🌿 **Dry roasting** – Bring out the subtle flavours of your whole spices by gently toasting them in a frying pan. When you can smell the aromas being released, take them off the heat and allow them to cool before grinding them.

🌿 **Frying** – For a more intense flavour, fry your whole spices in oil or ghee before adding the rest of the ingredients. The aromatic oils are released from the spices into the oil. Either leave whole in your curry for a subtler flavour or remove them, allow them to cool, then grind and put them back in the curry for a more intense hit.

🌿 **Tempering (tarka)** – Throw whole spices into very hot oil and allow them to sizzle. This creates an aromatic oil to pour over the finished curry as a dramatic garnish. Don't hold back on the garlic and chillies.

🌿 **Bhooning** – This traditional Indian cooking process, used in bhuna curries, involves heating the oil or ghee to smoking point then lowering the temperature and gently frying the spices with ginger, garlic and onions. This slow cooking produces a rich, silky gravy and allows the flavours to bind together.

Growing your own curry herbs and spices

Most herbs and spices for curry grow in hot or tropical countries, but many will grow in cooler climates if you have a warm spot in the garden or sunny windowsill. You need very little equipment – just a small trowel, plant pots and compost. Peat-free compost is environmentally friendly and has a looser texture, which helps seedlings send out roots.

In cooler areas, you can keep your seedlings warm in a propagator (a lidded incubator). Alternatively, use plastic egg boxes or upturned clear plastic fruit cartons over a tray of soil.

Growing your own is a fun way to have herbs and spices to hand when you're cooking; it's so rewarding to cook and eat home-grown produce that you may end up with a colourful mini-garden on your kitchen windowsill.

Tip: seeds are readily available from garden centres or online but you can also use the dried seeds you already have in your spice collection. For chillies, remove the seeds and dry them out for a few days before germinating.

GINGER

Ginger is an essential ingredient in most curries, but it's also known for its health benefits. A ginger infusion helps digestion and if partnered with cloves and honey in a hot lemon drink, it can soothe the symptoms of a cold.

To grow your own, choose a fresh, firm chunk of ginger with small nodules – this is the rhizome, the bulbous part of the root which produces new shoots. Submerge it in a bowl of warm water and within seven to ten days, you should see fine roots and green shoots.

Place it 3–4 cm deep, roots down, in a wide, shallow pot of compost and water it thoroughly. Cover it with a clear plastic bag and place on a sunny windowsill. Plant in early spring to give it the best chance of staying warm through the summer.

The new rhizomes take six to eight months to grow. Water little and often and you will be rewarded with an exotic plant not unlike bamboo, with long dark-green leaves which are also edible, although with a much milder ginger taste.

TURMERIC

Turmeric is an important addition to many curries and can be used fresh or dried. It is a member of the same family as ginger and is just as easy to grow. Although it is a hardy plant, it needs to be kept above 10°C (50°F). To get the rhizome to produce shoots, leave it in a warm, dry place. Once the shoots appear, follow the same growing instructions as for ginger (see page 51).

The turmeric plant produces large leaves which, once cooked, have a light, floral flavour. When raw, it is fresh and citrusy and fantastic grated onto salads.

You can also dry out the fresh rhizomes: wash them, slice as thinly as possible, put them in your oven on the very lowest setting until they are completely dry, then put the slices through a blender.

Beware: handling fresh turmeric *will* stain your chopping board and skin, but studies suggest that curcumin, the active ingredient, may be an effective anti-inflammatory, so there is some compensation for those bright yellow hands.

BAY LEAVES

This glossy-leaved evergreen is often used as a substitute for tej patta (Asian bay leaves). Originating from the Mediterranean, the bay tree loves sun and needs very little water yet is tough enough to endure temperatures down to –5°C (23°F).

Bay trees are available from garden centres, but you can easily grow your own by taking a cutting from an existing plant. Choose a clump of young leaves and snip off a small branch just above where the leaves are joined to the plant. Strip off all but a couple of the leaves and place in a small pot of compost and give it a good watering.

Bay trees naturally grow in an arid environment so keep it in a dry spot on a sunny windowsill. If you plant outdoors, wait until there is no danger of frost.

Fresh leaves have a richer flavour than dried. Add whole to dhals and rice dishes to add a subtle hint of warmth. The leaves are sharp-edged and inedible so it's best to remove them before serving.

TO BLITZ OR GRIND?

Ready-ground spices are the most convenient, but for that fresh, rich taste, buy whole ones and grind them yourself. A coffee bean grinder will easily do the job but for a more fun, authentic experience, use a mortar and pestle. A mortar is a bowl which holds the spices while you grind them with the club-shaped pestle.

Traditionally, Indian cooks would sit in front of a large, flat stone slab and use another hand-held stone as a pestle. To stop the spices drying out, the cook would periodically flick water over the mortar.

For the preparation of pastes for South East Asian curries, you can use a food processor or give your ingredients a good bashing with a mortar and pestle. It's a labour of love but many people say this is by far the best way to release those enticing aromas.

Nowadays, mortar and pestles come in a variety of sizes and materials; for spices, granite or marble are most effective.

GARLIC

Believed to have antibacterial and antifungal properties, and to lower cholesterol, this pungent bulb is an essential curry ingredient.

It's very easy to grow new garlic plants from a bulb and it's best to buy your bulbs from a garden centre or online, because these are treated to ensure they are certified disease-free. Cloves may be planted directly into the soil but it's much more fun to watch your garlic grow above ground. To do this, separate the cloves and stand them in a glass jar, pointed end up, in about a centimetre of water. Keep them wet and within a week your garlic cloves should have produced fine white roots and tall dark-green shoots.

Garlic will do well in a container on the windowsill, but it will also grow eagerly either in a pot or the ground. Plant it when the season is turning cold, as the drop in temperature stimulates the bulbs to grow. You will need to be patient – garlic can take up to ten months to grow.

CHILLIES

Chilli plants are readily available in supermarkets, but they are fun to grow from scratch and their shiny red or green fruits make an eye-catching addition to any kitchen windowsill.

For germination, your seeds will need a minimum of 15°C (59°F). A propagator with heat pad will give them a terrific boost, but you can plant them straight into the pot and cover with plastic. Gently pat them down into the compost, sprinkle a little more over the top and water them.

Germinate them during spring or, if you live in a colder climate, plant three to four months earlier and keep the seedlings in a warm place with the compost well drained. They need very little water. Depending on your local climate, the seedlings can take three to six months to produce fruit. When your plants are around 10 cm tall, they will need to be grown outside, where there are pollinating insects to help things along.

SAFFRON

Saffron strands are the stigmata of the dainty purple *Crocus sativus.* Each crocus produces just three stigmata, so it requires around 150 flowers to produce one gram of saffron, making it the world's most labour-intensive and expensive spice.

The good news is, if you have an outside space, you can grow your own very easily either in the ground or in pots. Make sure you buy bulbs for saffron crocus and not ordinary ones. Plant at the end of the summer. Place the bulbs 15 cm down and 10–15 cm apart. If your soil is very heavy, dig in some sharp sand to improve the drainage. The stigmata will be ready to harvest in autumn. Remove them carefully from the crocus with long tweezers and place them on kitchen roll in a warm place for a few days to dry out.

Tip: to coax maximum flavour and colour from saffron, soak it in milk, cream or water before use.

THREE DROPS OF BLOOD

In ancient Greek mythology, Hermes, winged messenger of the gods, fell in love with Krokos, a mortal youth. During discus practice one day, Hermes accidentally beheaded Krokos. Distraught, Hermes took three drops of blood from the head of his slain friend and turned them into stigmata, from which grew the saffron crocus.

The ancient Romans used the precious orange-gold strands of the saffron crocus to make perfume. Over the ages, the flower has also been used as a cure for melancholy, as a vivid yellow fabric dye, and as an offering to the gods.

CUMIN

Cumin seeds add a fantastic crunchy kick to salads and rice dishes as well as curries. You can purchase cumin seeds for cultivation but you can also grow plants from seeds you already have.

Soak the seeds in water for 24 hours, then plant them in a pot only lightly covered with compost. Within days you should have shoots which you can allow to grow into a tangle of slender sprouts. These make a great salad sprinkle.

If you want cumin seeds, you'll need to grow the plants outside. Germinate the seeds 10 cm apart and plant out when the seedlings are strong enough. Cumin needs consistent warmth, so it should be sown four weeks after the last frost has passed. It needs very little water; the compost should be almost dry before each watering.

Around 120 days after sowing, the cumin pods will turn brown and can be picked. Once harvested, break the pods over a colander placed inside a bowl. The seeds will slip through into the bowl, saving you from having to fiddle around to separate them.

MUSTARD

To produce the seeds for cooking, your plant will need to grow flowers, so it will need to be outside where there are pollinating insects to help things along.

Black and yellow seeds germinate equally well. They need a cool climate but plenty of light, so choose a sunny spot and sow a couple of weeks after the last frost. Sprinkle the seeds thinly, roughly 2 cm down, either in the ground or in large pots. Give them a good watering and they will eagerly germinate within 5-10 days and reach maturity in about six weeks.

The seeds will be ready when the slender pods are dry and yellow. Harvest them immediately before they burst of their own accord, otherwise the seeds will scatter far and wide and turn your garden into a mustard jungle the following year. To harvest the seeds, use the same colander and bowl method as for cumin (see page 59).

CORIANDER

Coriander plants thrive in well-watered pots on a warm, sunny windowsill, but if you want those fragrant seeds, as with the mustard plants (see page 60), you will need to grow it outside. If growing indoors, use pots around 20 cm deep.

Scatter the seeds over the compost and sprinkle a little more on top. After watering, cover with clear plastic or cling film and keep in a warm place. Make sure the compost stays moist. The seeds need three to five days to germinate. In cool climates, the plants may take a few months to reach the state of full maturity, which is when they produce seeds, but in warmer regions with temperatures over 25°C (77°F), they may only need four to six weeks.

If you specifically want the seeds, keep your coriander plants in bright sunlight – this should help them to bolt, i.e. shoot up without producing many leaves. To harvest the seeds, use the same colander and bowl method as for cumin (see page 59).

THE BIG NAMES

We're now going to look briefly at the characteristics and history of a few of the world's best-known curries. We'll explore these curries from a loosely geographical perspective, beginning with Indian dishes then branching out into South East Asia, followed by Japan and the Caribbean. We'll also look at some side dishes and accompaniments such as rice, chutneys and the variety of breads that are consumed with curry.

It's important to remember that curry has always been and always will be a moveable feast so although there are universally recognized dishes, there are no clearly defined and agreed recipes. Chefs in expensive restaurants, street-side vendors and ordinary people cooking in the family kitchen may all follow similar basic recipes, but they will tweak the heat levels, adjust the spices and sometimes even alter the cooking methods. In this way, they each put their own stamp on the dishes they produce, often leading to secret recipes, regional differences and friendly rivalry.

Vindaloo

This trailblazing curry began life as a very mild stew. When the Portuguese sailed to Goa, they took pork preserved in red wine and introduced the local people to *carne de vinha d'alhos*, a traditional Christmas dish from the island of Madeira in the Azores. This is pork marinated in red wine, vinegar, garlic, paprika and thyme, then pan-fried. During its time in Goa, this dish underwent a huge transformation.

Goan cooks replaced the wine with coconut toddy vinegar, the fermented sap of the coconut tree. The result was a sort of pickled effect. Ginger, tamarind, cinnamon, cumin, sugar and red Kashmiri chillies all entered the mix and *carne de vinha d'alhos* became the sour and tangy *vindalho* or *vindallo* which is still eaten at Christmas in Goa.

The version consumed in the West has undergone another fiery transformation with the addition of copious amounts of chillies. Unlike the original dish, vindaloo sometimes contains potatoes, as "alhos" was often mistaken for "aloo".

Tikka masala

Tender marinated chicken in a creamy gravy spiced with warm paprika, turmeric and cinnamon, tikka masala is a long-term favourite. An amusing story of its origin begins in an Indian restaurant in Glasgow during the 1970s when a customer is said to have lamented the dryness of his chicken curry. The chef took the offending dish back to the kitchen and coated it in tomato soup and cream (some accounts say yoghurt) and the customer was thereafter a happy man. This account has since been debunked and so the origins of tikka masala are still unclear. We do know that "tikka" refers to bite-sized chunks of meat. These were said to be favoured by the Mughal emperor Babur, who was afraid of choking on bones. The skewered meats, marinated in spiced yoghurt and cooked in a clay tandoor oven, became traditional to northern India, as did the mild, creamy murgh makhani (butter chicken). It would seem intuitive to combine these two dishes, so it's very possible that several chefs hit on the idea around the same time.

Balti

Balti is another dish whose origins are subject to grumbling disagreement. Some say it originated in northern India and Baltistan, in northern Pakistan, whereas others argue it was concocted in the cheap and cheerful curry houses of Birmingham, in the UK, during the 1980s.

The name is said to come from the Urdu word for "bucket", referring to the flat-bottomed wok-like pot in which baltis are commonly served.

A balti curry is a fusion of traditional recipes from Kashmir adapted to suit British tastes. It is heavy on the oil, garlic, tomatoes and onions, and a dash of juice or vinegar gives it a sharp tang. It is quickly cooked and in the balti dish on a high heat with fresh spices, usually ginger, turmeric, fenugreek and garam masala, with crunchy vegetables being added in the last 10 minutes. It usually contains meat but also works well with paneer or vegetables.

BREADS

🌿 **Naan bread** (see recipe on page 120) is leavened, traditionally with yoghurt, which tenderizes the gluten and helps the bread rise, giving it a pillowy texture. It is shaped by hand and slapped inside a tandoor oven, resulting in a smoky flavour. Ideal for scooping up curry and mopping up sauce. Traditionally a breakfast food.

🌿 **Roti** is a thin, unleavened flatbread, traditionally fried in a *tawa*, a flat griddle pan, which is traditionally made of stone. Roti has become a solid staple in all the areas that were populated by indentured workers.

🌿 A **chapati** is also unleavened but is made with wholemeal flour and contains oil or ghee. It is slapped from hand to hand (*chapat* is Hindi for "slap") then brushed with oil and griddled on a *tawa*.

🌿 Dense, chewy **paratha** bread is believed to have originated from the Punjab region of northern India and Pakistan. The dough is rolled out multiple times to create a flaky texture, before griddling on a *tawa*.

Korma

This popular but much maligned dish often strikes horror in the hearts of curry snobs; it is often seen as unadventurous and not a "proper" curry. The chicken and lamb kormas served in Western curry houses have very little heat, often none at all, and can be quite sweet and creamy, but korma has a long history and there are other variations on the recipe not normally seen in the West.

To understand korma we need to go back to those Mughals in their palaces, where it was a favourite dish of theirs. Meat or vegetables would be dropped into a pan of hot ghee, then quickly sautéed on a high heat before being slow-cooked in a sealed pot (*qorma* is Urdu for "braise") containing yoghurt with garlic, ginger and spices such as coriander, mace and cardamom. For special celebrations, ground almonds and sultanas would be added, along with cream, to make a white korma, a truly luxurious dish.

It is said that great dishes of white korma decorated with silver leaf were served to Shah Jahan and his guests at the opening of the Taj Mahal in the seventeenth century – an extravagant white curry for an extravagant white mausoleum.

There are many local variants of korma but, broadly speaking, they can be split into three main types. Those from southern India and Malaysia contain coconut milk, tomatoes and hotter spices, while the decadent north Indian version contains fragrant spices, yoghurt, cashew nuts, almonds and sometimes cream. In contrast, the perkier Kashmiri kormas contain fennel seeds, tamarind and the cockscomb flowers that are used to give rogan josh its red colour.

A nineteenth-century Indian cookery book, published in Calcutta, describes korma as "one of the richest of Hindoostanee curries, quite unsuited to European taste". Clearly, it has grown on Europeans since then.

Jalfrezi

Jalfrezi originates from Bengal, most likely from Kolkata, or Calcutta as it was known at that time when it was the centre of the British Raj. The Chinese-influenced jalfrezi is stir-fried, so it is a dry curry.

The wealthy households during the Raj were pretty extravagant and wasted a lot of food. Many Indians had been forced into poverty by British rule so they would use up the leftover vegetables and roast meats. With the addition of spices and garlic and a quick toss in the pan, the scraps would be transformed into a tasty curry. In fact, jalfrezi made an appearance in Anglo-Indian recipe books at that time.

A modern jalfrezi typically involves marinating the meats in spiced yoghurt then stir-frying with onions, ginger, garlic, tomatoes and peppers. It is quite a tangy curry due to the tomatoes and peppers. A jalfrezi is still a great way to transform leftovers into a curry; as it is stir-fried, it's perfect for vegetables, paneer and chickpeas.

Lassi

Lassi is a chilled yoghurt drink. It has been around for thousands of years and originated in the Punjab (northern India and eastern Pakistan). It is chilled and astringent, which makes it the perfect accompaniment to a hot curry.

Historically, lassi consisted of yoghurt, ice and salt, but nowadays lassi may be sweet or salty and there are many variations on this refreshing drink. This recipe is for mango lassi, but if you would like to make yours salty, simply miss out the mango, limes, cardamom and sugar/honey and add a dash of salt.

INGREDIENTS

2 mangoes, peeled and de-stoned

250 g natural yoghurt (use Greek if you want extra creaminess)

50 ml chipped ice

Juice of ½–1 lime

Sugar or honey to taste

Pinch of ground cardamom

Blitz all the ingredients in a blender until frothy. Garnish with a pinch of chopped pistachio nuts or a few strands of saffron.

Biryani

Meat in a spiced yoghurt marinade, saffron rice, crisped onions, sour plums, toasted almonds and splashes of rose water: this star-studded cast of ingredients is a dish fit for a king, or in this case, a Mughal emperor.

In the bustling kitchens of Mughal palaces, a team of Persian chefs would be on standby in case they were needed to cook up a sumptuous banquet at a moment's notice. The practice of cooking rice and meat in a tightly sealed clay pot called a *dum pukht* originated from the mountains of central Asia, but it was in these palaces that the dish was glammed up by the fusion of spiced meats with pilaf, a Persian rice dish of nuts and dried fruits.

Biryani is a dish that can be as fancy or simple as time and resources allow, so although it is commonly served at wedding banquets and celebrations, a simplified version can also be cooked for everyday consumption.

The meat is tenderized with a generous quantity of richly spiced yoghurt. Spices commonly used are ginger, cumin, coriander, red chilli powder and cardamom. The meat is then layered with tomatoes, crisped onions and par-cooked pilau rice.

The biryani may be cooked in the oven in a lidded casserole dish (Dutch oven), but a large sealed pan on the stove top will do just as well. The moisture from the yoghurt and tomato rises up and cooks the rice, infusing it with flavours.

Traditionally, biryani would have been cooked with mutton, but nowadays it can be lamb, chicken or vegetables. Different variations exist all over the world, and within India there is some rivalry between cities. Hyderabadi biryani, for example, is richly spiced while the Kolkata version is milder and features boiled eggs and potatoes.

Dhansak

This slow-cooked, highly spiced, bubbling cauldron of a dish originates from Persia and is thought to be a derivation of khoresh, a meat and lentil stew containing plums and spinach. It is believed to have been taken to India during the eighth and tenth centuries by Zoroastrians fleeing religious persecution, who sailed across the Arabian Sea and landed on the shores of Gujarat on the west coast.

The evolved dish, known as dhansak, became popular at the end of the nineteenth century when the growth of the cities of Mumbai and Karachi attracted more Persian immigrants who set up street stalls selling it along with chai and hot snacks.

Traditionally, dhansak is a lentil-thickened, goat or mutton dish, although a modern dhansak can contain chicken or prawns. It typically contains potatoes and aubergines. Pumpkin or squash lends it some sweetness, while tomatoes, tamarind or lime juice are balanced with sugar to give it a unique sweet-sour robustness. This was a very mild dish originally, but over time the spicy influence of Gujarati cuisine crept in.

Today it is hot, rich and aromatic due to an abundance of sweet spices such as ground ginger, nutmeg, coriander seeds, cardamom and cloves. Sticky, caramelized onion rice is a common accompaniment and, for contrast, the curry is often served with crunchy condiments such as a salty salad of tomatoes, cucumber and red onions doused in vinegar.

The 6 or 7 hours of preparation and cooking time required for the simplest dhansak may make it seem like a true labour of love, but the richly satisfying nature of this dish ensures its universal popularity and many families will fiercely guard their secret recipe.

Dhansak is very much a communal dish. In India, it is often eaten on a Sunday due to the length of time it takes for the lentils and meat to cook. A family may also cook this to mark the end of four days of mourning after the death of a family member, during which no meat would be eaten.

Rogan josh

Rogan josh is from Kashmir but it was taken there by the Mughals who would retreat to the cool mountains and fresh flowing rivers to escape the searing summer heat. It is an important feature of the *wazwan,* a Kashmiri feast for special occasions such as a marriage or birth.

Mutton or goat would be cooked slowly with garlic, ghee and aromatic spices such as cinnamon, cardamom and cloves. The distinctive red colour of this richly flavoured dish may come from a few sources. Traditionally, the cockscomb flower, which resembles the crest of a cockerel, would be used. Another pigment-imparting ingredient is ratan jot, an ordinary-looking piece of bark which turns brilliant red when stirred into hot oil.

In the West, these ingredients are not usually easy to get hold of so powdered Kashmiri chillies are used. Unlike western adaptations, the traditional version of this dry curry does not contain tomatoes.

POPPADUMS (POPPADOMS)

However you spell them, these universally adored, crispy accompaniments are made by forming dough from flour, water and sometimes spices before shaping it into discs and deep-frying. The Hindi phrase *papad belna* literally translates as "rolling out papad". Over time, it has become a common phrase to describe putting in a great effort. More fancifully, and more reflective of the papad-making process, *papad belna* could be seen as going through fire and water to complete a task.

Thali

Thali originated in India. It consists of several small dishes of food served at the same time. In northern India, a metal plate is used (*thali* is Hindi for "plate") and in the south, thali is served on a banana leaf, which is believed to be antibacterial.

Thali consists of a carbohydrate, usually chapati or roti in the north of India or rice in the south. This sits in the middle of the tray with the smaller dishes, or *kothari*, arranged around it.

There can be anything between five of these, which would be pretty modest, and 15 for special occasions and celebrations.

There are many regional variations, depending on availability of ingredients and eating customs in that area. For example, in Gujarat, in the west of India, the thali is very elaborate, consisting of vegetables cooked in ghee, fried snacks and desserts. Maharashtra, also in western India, is famous for its broth and spiced mutton thali.

Variations in the practice of serving a variety of small portions at the same time can be found in other countries, such as the Balinese *rijsttafel* (rice table). A gluttonous throwback to the Dutch colonial era, this involved anything up to 40 dishes with as wide a range of tastes and textures as possible. Nowadays *rijsttafel* is only served in a small handful of tourist restaurants.

In Mauritius, the traditional *sept cari,* or "seven curries", originates from migrants and Indian indentured workers, mostly from Tamil Nadu in southern India. A selection of seven dishes is served on plantain leaves and typically includes a sweet, milky dessert; a fried, sweet dumpling; a tamarind soup; and *cari zak,* spiced jackfruit. *Sept cari* is always served at celebrations, festivals and weddings. Both Mauritian *sept cari* and Indian thali derive from the Ayurvedic principle of including in every meal the correct balance of all six tastes of sweet, salt, bitter, sour, astringent and spicy.

Dhal

Dhal (or dal) is a dried, split pulse such as lentils, chickpeas, split peas or beans, but the cooked dish is also referred to as dhal. There are references to dhal in ancient Indian texts dating as far back as 300 BCE, when lentils were a staple food in the civilization of the Indus Valley. They remain so today and are eaten all over the world, particularly in the areas where indentured labourers were sent.

Dhal is a comforting, stick-to-your-ribs dish which, when cooked slowly with ghee, takes on a silky texture. It is so versatile it can be used for soups and curries or to fill roti. Its mild flavour means it pairs well with just about any spice you care to put in it, but particularly good ones are black cardamom, red chillies and cumin. Without question, the most glorious finishing touch to a steaming bowl of dhal is a pool of tarka: hot, spiced oil or ghee.

Aloo gobi

Aloo gobi is a potato and cauliflower dish. Only very small amounts of liquid are added during the cooking process, resulting in a dry, highly spiced delight. It originates from the Punjab, but this cheap, filling and comforting dish is widely eaten throughout India and Pakistan and of course in curry houses throughout the world.

Compared to more traditional dishes such as biryani or korma, aloo gobi is a relative newcomer to Indian cuisine because it is the pairing of two imports: potatoes from the Portuguese and cauliflower from the British. Both these ingredients have a mild taste, and because they readily absorb other flavours, they are perfect for this beautifully spiced dish. Ginger, turmeric, cumin, coriander and garlic are the classic spices in aloo gobi, with the turmeric giving it its mild yellow colour. It is often sprinkled with nigella seeds (black cumin).

THE INDIA WAY

Hannah Glasse's *The Art of Cookery Made Plain and Easy,* published in 1747, was the first Western recipe book to feature curry. The adventurous recipe, entitled "To Make a Currey the India Way", was delicately spiced with turmeric, ground black pepper, ginger and lemon juice. You can almost hear and smell it bubbling away on the cast iron cooking ranges in elegant Georgian houses.

Thai curry

The starting point for Thai curries is a paste with a multitude of aromatic ingredients such as chillies, garlic, coriander, shallots, lemongrass, lime leaves, ginger and galangal. These are pounded or blitzed together, then either fried to release the aromas or added to the curry with coconut milk.

The key to obtaining those bright, tangy flavours is getting the right balance. Sour ingredients such as lime juice are countered by the sweetness of coconut milk and palm sugar, and the whole lot is grounded by an umami (savoury) ingredient such as soy sauce or shrimp paste.

Thai curries may be red, green or yellow. The paste for red curries contains red chillies, coriander and lime zest. This fiery, salty paste is a good all-rounder for meat, fish or vegetables. Green curry paste contains green chillies, lime leaves and basil, while turmeric gives yellow paste its colour – it contains coriander and cumin seeds and is great for fish and seafood curries.

Rendang

Rendang is a dark, intensely spiced curry. Originating from Sumatra, this robust beef stew enjoys a global popularity. The dry texture of rendang is similar to the curries of northern India, so it's most likely it was introduced by Indian merchants to Indonesia.

When Minang traders from the highlands of north-west Sumatra began to travel by rivers and sea to what is now the Malaysian peninsula, they needed a way to transport food. They adopted the Indian method of slow-cooking beef in spices which they would then dry out, so it could be stored on their boats and rehydrated as needed.

The Minang used the tropical ingredients of coconut milk, star anise, lime leaves and lemongrass, although rendang contains ginger, red chillies and garlic in common with Indian curries. The cooking process would traditionally take 6 or 7 hours and this is thought by Minang people to reflect the virtues of wisdom, patience and persistence.

Massaman

Mildly hot, intensely spiced and with a hard-to-master balance of sweet, salty and sour, massaman combines the best of Persian, Indian and Thai cuisine.

Beef or chicken are slow-cooked in coconut milk with a dense, dark paste of toasted, fragrant spices. Chopped peanuts are added to create an interesting texture, then orange or pineapple juice is squeezed in at the end to add some sweet-sour notes.

The dish is believed to have been introduced to Thailand from Malaysia around the seventeenth century by Persian merchants. In fact, the word "massaman" comes from *Mosalman,* meaning Muslim. However, Princess Bunrod of Thailand, future wife of Prince Itsarasunthon (who went on to become King Rama II), is believed by some to have been responsible for the fusion of styles seen in massaman curry. The prince loved this dish so much he mentioned it in a poem he wrote in 1800 in homage to his beloved:

> *Massaman, the jewel in my eyes*
> *With fragrant cumin and spicy flavour*
> *Any man who tastes her curry*
> *Can't help but dream about her.*

Japanese curry

Japanese curry is a savoury, slightly sweet dish. It's mildly spiced, with a comforting stew-like texture, possibly not so dissimilar to those vats of curry cooked up for the British and Japanese military (see page 34). It has become as versatile as it is popular and is sold as fast food, cooked by families, served in top restaurants and eagerly devoured by hungry children in school canteens.

The starting point for Japanese curry is a block of curry roux: a mix of fat and flour with added spices. It will typically contain turmeric, cumin, fenugreek and coriander but there are hundreds of variations available. The curry usually contains onions, potatoes and carrots and with apples or honey added as a sweetening agent and it is often accompanied by pickles or boiled eggs. It may be served with rice, noodles or bread. It has even been stuffed inside savoury doughnuts. Considering the refined, well-presented dishes usually associated with Japanese cuisine, it is possible the sloppy texture and comforting warmth of this curry makes a welcome change.

Curry goat

Mutton curry was introduced to the Caribbean by Indians from Uttar Pradesh in northern India, where it is a staple. The more commonly available goat took the place of mutton in the Caribbean and today curry goat is a quintessential dish of the Caribbean islands, in particular Jamaica.

Caribbean curries tend to be made using curry powder containing a blend of savoury notes from cumin and turmeric, balanced with distinctively sweet spices such as coriander, mustard, star anise, fenugreek and, most importantly, allspice (dried, sweet pimento berries) and Scotch bonnet chillies. The meat is marinated with a spice rub containing such items as curry powder, garlic, salt and oil, then slow-cooked with onions, carrots, potato, ginger, garlic, cumin, black pepper, Scotch bonnet and perhaps a splash of rum. Herbs commonly associated with European cooking – such as parsley, thyme, bay leaves and chives – may also be added, together with shado beni, the nearest Caribbean equivalent to spinach.

BUSS-UP SHUT

In Trinidad and Tobago, paratha bread is a legacy of indentured labourers from India. It has evolved over the years to become a layered, buttery flatbread and is commonly served as a side to dishes such as aloo (potato curry), chana (chickpea curry) and curry goat. This silky heap of flaky bread is known as "buss-up shut" because of its resemblance to a torn and messed-up (bust-up) shirt.

COOKING
CURRY

With so many spices and ingredients available, and the huge range of recipes out there, the prospect of cooking your own curry might seem a little daunting, but it need not be. Here we have a selection of the most popular curries with basic, easy-to-follow recipes. They vary from very simple to a little more complex, but they should all be fun to try out.

If you're new to cooking curry, keep it simple to begin with: a humble dhal or aloo gobi can be just as satisfying as a fancy biryani. Remember to taste, sniff and tweak your curry as you go along, particularly towards the end of the cooking process.

It's important not to be a slave to the recipe; feel free to leave out any spices or ingredients you're not keen on and add more of those you like. This is your curry and a big part of the enjoyment is putting your own personal stamp on it. All recipes serve four people.

Top tips for cooking curry

🌿 Always use fresh garlic and ginger. If in doubt, use equal quantities.

🌿 For that special tarka or biryani, or for sheer indulgence, use pure ghee.

🌿 Never let your spices burn. One way to prevent this is to put vegetable oil in with your butter or ghee. Stir frequently. Keep a little water to hand and add in small amounts if necessary. If you do burn your spices, discard and start again, otherwise that bitter taste will cling stubbornly to your curry all the way to your broken-hearted taste buds.

🌿 If you're using lemongrass, cut off the root end and peel away the first three or four tough outer layers until the lemongrass is slightly pliable.

🌿 If you're cooking for a group of people, serve a separate dish of finely chopped red chillies. Those who like it fiery can sprinkle this over their curry.

🌿 For vegetarian options, use Indian paneer cheese which is robust enough for cooking and pairs very well with spinach. Tofu, tempeh, beans, nuts (cashews work well in curry) and chickpeas are all tasty vegan alternatives.

Conversions

The recipes in this chapter use metric measurements, but if you prefer using imperial (and you don't have a smartphone to do the conversions for you), here are some basic tables:

25 g ≈ 1 oz	15 ml ≈ ½ fl. oz
60 g ≈ 2 oz	30 ml ≈ 1 fl. oz
85 g ≈ 3 oz	75 ml ≈ 2½ fl. oz
115 g ≈ 4 oz	120 ml ≈ 4 fl. oz
255 g ≈ 9 oz	270 ml ≈ 9 fl. oz

Cooking curry

MAIN
DISHES

Lamb or chicken bhuna

This slow-cooked dish has a rich flavour and a silky texture.

INGREDIENTS

2 large onions, finely chopped

1 tsp salt

2 tbsp oil or ghee

4 garlic cloves, crushed

4 tsp finely chopped ginger

1 tsp ground turmeric

2 tsp chilli powder

2 tsp coriander

2 tsp cumin powder

2 tsp curry powder

2 green chillies, chopped

4 chopped tomatoes/1 tin chopped tomatoes

4 chicken breast fillets, diced or 500g lamb, diced (for vegan alternative, use a can of chickpeas)

Handful of fresh coriander, chopped

In a frying pan or wok, fry the onion with the salt in the ghee or oil until soft and golden.

Reduce the heat and add the garlic and ginger. After a few minutes, add a little hot water and cook until the ingredients are soft and creamy.

Add the spices, cook on a high heat for a few minutes then reduce the heat, add the chillies and tomatoes and cook for a few minutes.

Add the meat and stir occasionally until it's cooked through and brown. Alternatively, add the chickpeas. You will need to add a little water at this point to prevent burning.

Cover and cook gently until the water has evaporated and the meat/chickpeas are coated in a thick, silky sauce – approximately 20–30 minutes.

Garnish with the coriander and serve with pilau rice or naan bread and raita (see page 115) or lime pickle (see page 122).

Paneer jalfrezi

A perky, cheerful stir-fry curry which is quick and simple to make.

INGREDIENTS

1 tsp cumin seeds
3 tbsp vegetable oil
1 medium onion, chopped into large pieces
3 cloves of garlic, crushed
1 tsp chilli powder
1 tsp ground coriander
½ tsp ground turmeric
1 medium green pepper, chopped into large pieces
1 large tomato, cut into wedges
2 tsp crushed ginger
1 tbsp lemon juice
230 g paneer, diced
Salt to taste
Handful of fresh coriander, chopped

Fry the cumin seeds in the oil for 30 seconds. Use a deep frying pan.

Fry the onion until it becomes transparent then add the garlic and cook for a few more seconds.

Stir in the remaining spices for a minute (you may need to add a splash of water to stop the spices sticking to the pan).

Stir in the pepper and cook for a further 5 minutes.

Add the tomato and ginger and cook until the tomatoes start to soften.

Add the paneer and cook for a few minutes to allow it to become coated with the spices.

Stir in the lemon juice.

Add the coriander garnish and serve with rice or naan bread. Savoury poppadoms contrast well with this tangy stir-fry.

Sri Lankan coconut and pineapple curry

A spicy, fruity curry that will take you straight to the tropics.

INGREDIENTS

1 large onion, sliced

3–4 tbsp oil

1 tsp mustard seeds

3 garlic cloves, crushed

2 tsp ginger, crushed

1 tsp fennel seeds

1–2 tsp chilli powder

1 tsp powdered turmeric

½ tsp cinnamon

4 cardamom pods, crushed

1 sprig of curry leaves (if unavailable, use a squirt of lemon)

1 medium-large pineapple, skinned and cubed

½–¾ tin coconut milk

Salt and sugar to taste

Handful of fresh coriander, chopped

1–2 red chillies, deseeded and finely chopped (optional)

Fry the onion in the oil until just beginning to turn golden. Stir in the mustard seeds and fry for a minute.

Stir in the garlic, ginger and the rest of the spices and fry for a few minutes.

Stir in the pineapple, put the lid on the pan and simmer on a low heat for 5-10 minutes, stirring occasionally as the juice comes out of the pineapple.

Add the coconut milk and simmer for a further 15-20 minutes.

Season with salt and/or sugar to taste and garnish with the chopped coriander (coriander and pineapple really are a match made in heaven) and, if desired, the chopped red chillies.

Serve as a side dish to a savoury beef curry or as a dish in its own right with fluffy white rice.

Tarka dhal

This grounding, savoury lentil curry makes a great winter warmer.

INGREDIENTS

2 tbsp ghee or butter and vegetable oil

1 large onion, finely sliced

1 tsp mustard seeds

2 tsp garlic, crushed

1 tsp fresh ginger, finely grated

1 tsp cumin seeds

½ tsp turmeric

1½ tsp chilli powder

1 black cardamom pod

200 g red lentils

1 tbsp tomato puree

Salt to taste

2 large tomatoes, peeled and chopped

1 tbsp lemon juice

1½ tsp garam masala

Handful of fresh coriander, chopped

Heat half the ghee or butter and oil mix to a high temperature. Set a tablespoon of onion to one side and fry the rest for a few minutes.

Add the mustard seeds, cover the pan with a lid and fry until the seeds begin to pop. Take the pan off the heat and wait until the seeds have finished popping before removing the lid. Put back on the heat, add the garlic, ginger and cumin seeds and fry for a minute or two.

Add the turmeric, 1 tsp of the chilli powder, black cardamom, lentils, tomato puree and enough water to cover the lentils with a couple of extra centimetres to spare. Add salt and simmer for 10 minutes. You may need to add more water to stop the lentils drying up. It's up to you how solid or runny you want your dhal to be.

Stir in the fresh tomatoes, lemon juice and 1 tsp of the garam masala and simmer until the lentils are cooked. If you prefer a smooth texture, use a hand-held blender or a potato masher to break the lentils down.

Stir the coriander into the mixture or use it for a garnish.

In a separate pan, bring the rest of the ghee to a high heat and fry the remainder of the onion. Just as the onion becomes crisp and golden, reduce the heat and stir in the rest of the garam masala and chilli powder.

Pour this over the top of the dhal before serving. This spiced oil is optional but it adds a terrific hit of flavour to your dhal.

This robust savoury dish goes perfectly with a tangy raita and pilau rice or naan bread.

Japanese katsu curry

This thick, savoury curry pairs beautifully with the katsu (crispy fried chicken).

INGREDIENTS

For the curry:

1 large onion, cut into 1 cm chunks

1 large potato, cut into 1 cm chunks

1 large carrot, cut into 1 cm chunks

800 ml water

3–5 cubes Japanese curry roux (available in most supermarkets)

Half a sweet apple, finely grated

For the katsu:

2 chicken breasts, sliced horizontally to create 4 thin, flat cutlets

5 tbsp plain flour

1 egg, beaten

100 g panko breadcrumbs*

Salt and pepper for seasoning

Vegetable oil

Put the chopped vegetables into a large saucepan half-filled with boiling water. Turn down to simmer until vegetables are just about soft.

Add the curry roux and continue to simmer for 10 minutes. Keep stirring until the curry has thickened then add the grated apple.

Season the chicken pieces with salt and pepper then coat with flour. Dip the chicken into the egg and then the breadcrumbs until thoroughly coated. For extra crispiness, give your chicken pieces a second dip in the egg and breadcrumbs.

Deep fry the chicken cutlets in a deep frying pan – a few minutes on each side until golden brown.

Cut the chicken katsu into slices and serve with the sauce and sticky Japanese rice. Boiled egg halves and Japanese pickled radish make great garnishes.

---

*Either buy panko breadcrumbs ready-made or make your own by blitzing white bread in the food processor then toasting them on a low heat for 30–40 minutes.

Vegetable balti

This recipe is traditionally cooked in a stainless steel balti dish, but an ordinary frying pan will do.

INGREDIENTS

For the paste:
4 garlic cloves, crushed

2 tsp ginger, crushed

1–2 tsp chilli powder

1–2 tsp ground cinnamon

1 tbsp ground cumin

1 tbsp ground coriander

1 tbsp ground cardamom

1 tbsp garam masala

3 tbsp tomato puree

50 ml water

For the balti:
2 tbsp ghee or vegetable oil

1 large onion, thinly sliced

½ cauliflower head, cut into small florets

½ butternut squash, peeled and cut into 2 cm chunks

1 red pepper, deseeded and cut into 2 cm chunks

1 green pepper, deseeded and cut into 2 cm chunks

4–5 large chopped tomatoes

300–400 ml water

100 g frozen peas

Zest and juice of
  1 lime

Salt and pepper
  to taste

Sugar (optional)

2 handfuls of fresh
  coriander

Blend the paste ingredients and water together in a food processor.

Gently fry the onion in a wok or frying pan until translucent.

Add the paste and cook for 2 or 3 minutes. You may need to add a little more water to prevent the spices burning.

Stir in the cauliflower, butternut squash and peppers, ensuring all the vegetables are coated in the spice mixture.

Add the tomatoes and water then simmer until the vegetables are cooked, approximately 15–20 minutes.

Stir in the peas and cook for 3 minutes then add the lime, salt and pepper (if desired) and one handful of the fresh coriander.

This is quite a tangy recipe, so give it a taste – you may need to counteract the acidity with a little sugar.

Garnish with the rest of the fresh coriander and serve with rice or naan bread and a salty pickle.

Aloo gobi

A simple, traditional dish which is suitable for a main course or as a tasty side dish.

INGREDIENTS

4–6 tbsp oil

1 tsp cumin seeds

1 large onion, roughly chopped

3–4 medium potatoes, diced

1 medium cauliflower, cut into florets
(include the stalks and cut slightly larger
than the potatoes)

4–6 garlic cloves, crushed

1 tbsp ginger, grated

5 fresh tomatoes, chopped

½–1 tsp chilli powder

2 tsp ground coriander

½ tsp turmeric

½ tsp salt

2–4 green chillies (optional)

2 tsp garam masala

Fresh lemon juice

2 handfuls of fresh coriander, chopped

Heat the oil in a wok or frying pan to a medium-high heat.

Fry the cumin seeds for half a minute or so then add the onion and fry until they begin to turn golden brown.

Transfer the onion to a bowl and fry the cauliflower and potato. You may need to add more oil first. Once golden brown, transfer this to a separate bowl.

Turn the heat down to medium and add the onion and cumin seeds.

Stir in the garlic and ginger and cook for a couple of minutes. You may need to add a little water at this point to prevent burning. Keep stirring.

Add the tomatoes, chilli powder, coriander, turmeric and half a teaspoon of salt. If using green chillies, add them now. Return the cauliflower and potatoes to the pan, cover and simmer until they are cooked.

Stir in the garam masala and cook for a few more minutes, then remove from the heat and stir in half the fresh coriander and lemon juice.

Use the rest of the fresh coriander for garnish.

Serve with naan bread or roti and lime pickle (see page 122).

Beef rendang

A dark, aromatic beef and coconut curry.

INGREDIENTS

For the paste:

5 shallots

6 cloves of garlic

3 cm ginger

3 cm galangal (if not available, use 5 cm ginger instead and add a generous squirt of lime)

3 lemongrass stalks (remove a couple of the harder, outer layers)

10 deseeded red chillies, medium heat

For the curry:

5 tbsp cooking oil

1 cinnamon stick

4 star anise

4 crushed cardamom pods

600 g stewing beef

2 crushed lemongrass stalks

250 ml coconut milk

2 tsp tamarind paste

250 ml water
6–8 finely shredded lime leaves
6–8 tbsp kerisik*
1 tbsp sugar

Blend the paste ingredients in a food processor.

Heat the oil, add the spice paste, cinnamon, star anise and cardamom and fry until the spice aromas are released.

Add beef, lemongrass, coconut milk, tamarind and water. Simmer until the meat is cooked. Add lime leaves, kerisik and sugar, then simmer for 60–90 minutes until the sauce has reduced.

Serve with fluffy rice cooked in coconut milk and, if desired, add a spoonful of sambal (see page 118).

*Kerisik is freshly grated coconut, toasted and pounded. Alternatively, gently brown 6-8 tbsp of coconut cream in a pan.

Jamaican curry goat

Scotch bonnet is *extremely* hot. If you don't want your curry to be too fierce, omit this ingredient.

INGREDIENTS

900 g goat meat, chopped (alternatively, use stewing lamb)
1 medium onion, diced
2 tsp minced garlic
4 tbsp Jamaican curry powder*
1 tsp black pepper
1 Scotch bonnet pepper, deseeded and sliced
Salt to taste
1 tsp allspice
1 tbsp turmeric
4 tbsp vegetable oil
3–4 generous sprigs of thyme
1 medium carrot, diced
1 medium potato, diced
1 tbsp coconut cream (optional)

In a mixing bowl, combine the meat with the onion, garlic, Jamaican curry powder, black pepper, scotch bonnet, allspice and turmeric, ensuring the meat is well coated. Leave to marinate, ideally for 24 hours, otherwise allow 1-2 hours.

Heat the oil in a saucepan and add the meat. Keep stirring while you allow it to brown. You may need to add a little water to stop it burning.

Add the thyme and enough hot water to cover the meat and simmer for a couple of hours until the meat is tender.

Add the carrots and potatoes approximately 30 minutes before the end.

Stir in the optional tablespoon of coconut cream for added richness.

Serve with Jamaican rice and peas or with roti.

*Most supermarkets stock this but if you can't get hold of it, use ordinary curry powder and add extra allspice (pimento) or blend your own substitute (see page 39 in the Spice 101 section).

Cambodian prawn amok

A hot, fragrant prawn curry which is both light and simple.

INGREDIENTS

For the paste:

5 shallots, chopped

4 lemongrass stalks, chopped (remove a few of
the tough outer layers)

6 garlic cloves

1–2 red chillies

2 tsp turmeric

2 tbsp ginger

Zest of 2 limes

6–8 lime leaves

2 tsp salt

2 tsp sugar

For the curry:

2 tbsp vegetable oil

200 g fine green beans, split lengthways

2 pak choi, chopped

2 cans of coconut milk

1–2 tbsp fish sauce

1 tsp sugar
500 g raw, peeled prawns
Handful of mint, chopped
Handful of Thai basil, chopped

Blitz the paste ingredients in a food processor or pound using a mortar and pestle.

Stir-fry the paste in the oil for a couple of minutes.

Add the beans, pak choi and coconut milk and simmer for 10-15 minutes.

Add the fish sauce and sugar. At this point, it's a good idea to taste and make sure you're happy with the savoury-sweet balance.

Add the prawns and simmer until they are cooked – roughly 5-7 minutes.

Add the mint and basil.

This dish has enough flavour to be served in a bowl as a refreshing curry. Alternatively, pair with jasmine rice.

Cooking curry

SIDE DISHES

Raita

This zesty yet cooling yoghurt side is a fantastic accompaniment to any savoury curry, particularly dhal.

INGREDIENTS

¼ cucumber
250 ml full fat yoghurt
¼ tsp cumin seeds, dry toasted
Few sprigs of coriander, chopped
Few sprigs of mint, chopped
Pinch of garam masala
1 clove of garlic, crushed
Pinch of chilli (optional)

Scoop the seeds out of the cucumber and finely slice or grate the skin and flesh. Combine all the ingredients in a bowl and add a pinch of salt.

Pilau rice

This yellow, mildly spiced rice is traditionally served with Indian curries.

INGREDIENTS

40 g ghee or butter and oil
1 large onion, finely sliced (optional)
½ tsp mustard seeds
¾ tsp cumin seeds
4 crushed cardamom pods
Small stick of cinnamon
3–4 cloves
2 bay leaves
1 tsp ground turmeric
300 g basmati rice, well rinsed
600 ml water
Salt to taste

Gently heat the ghee or butter and oil and fry the onion until beginning to brown. Add the mustard seeds, put a lid on the pan and fry until the seeds begin to pop.

Take the pan off the heat, wait until the seeds have finished popping before removing the lid then put back on the heat, adding the cumin seeds, crushed cardamom pods, cinnamon, cloves, bay leaves and turmeric.

Cook the spices and onion on a gentle heat for a minute or two, then add the rice, stirring it in well.

Add the water and a pinch of salt. Bring to the boil, then turn down. Cover and simmer until the water has been absorbed and the rice is almost cooked – roughly 8-10 minutes. You might need to add a little more water to prevent it drying out.

Add dots of butter if desired, replace the lid and leave for 5 minutes before serving to allow the rice to fluff up.

Sambal

Sambal is an earthy chilli paste, popular in Malaysia and Indonesia. This condiment can also be used as a base for South East Asian coconut curries.

INGREDIENTS

20–30 dried chillies, washed and soaked in hot water until soft (usually half an hour or so)

10–12 shallots

6 cloves of garlic

6 lime leaves

5 stalks of lemongrass (remove a few of the tough outer layers)

20 g ginger

15 g fresh turmeric

3–5 tbsp tamarind paste

2–3 tbsp sugar

Salt to taste

Vegetable oil

Remove the chilli stems and seeds. If you want more bang in your sambal, leave the seeds in.

Put all the ingredients except the tamarind, sugar and salt into a food processor or mortar.

Add a slug of oil, then blitz or pound to a paste and fry gently for 15 minutes or so in 15–20 tbsp of oil.

Add the tamarind, sugar and salt, then fry for 5 minutes or until the paste is a dark red-brown.

Once cool, transfer to a jar. Sambal will keep for up to a week in the fridge.

Serve as a side with any Thai or creamy curry.

Naan bread

This classic, all-purpose staple is a great accompaniment to any curry.

INGREDIENTS

1 sachet dried yeast (7 g)
2 tsp caster sugar
125 ml warm water in a bowl
300 g strong white bread flour
½ tsp salt
½ tsp baking powder
25 g melted butter, plus extra to brush the pan and glaze the breads
150 ml natural yoghurt

Add the yeast and 1 tsp of the sugar to the bowl of warm water and leave until frothy (approximately 15 minutes).

In another bowl, mix the flour with the rest of the sugar, salt and baking powder and make a well in the middle.

Pour the melted butter, yeast mixture and yoghurt into the well. Stir everything together with a spoon then, using your hands, bring the ingredients together into a ball.

At this stage, adjust by adding a little more water if the mixture is too dry, or flour if it's too wet.

Knead the dough on a floured surface for 10 minutes or so. It should feel soft and elastic.

Place the ball of dough into a buttered bowl, cover with a cloth and leave for an hour. The dough should double in size during this time.

Divide the dough into four to six balls, depending on how large you want them, then place on a flour-dusted baking tray and cover with a damp cloth.

Roll out one of the balls of dough and place in a dry, non-stick frying pan which has been preheated to a high temperature.

Fry the bread for 4 minutes or so on each side. It should bubble and puff up.

As you cook each bread, brush with melted butter and sprinkle with a little salt (optional) then keep them warm in the oven, preheated to its lowest setting. Cover with foil to keep them moist.

Lime pickle

This hot sour pickle is fabulous with anything.

INGREDIENTS

7 limes (thin-skinned
limes are best) cut
into small chunks

85 g salt

2 tsp cumin seeds

2 tsp fennel seeds

2 tsp mustard seeds

1 tsp fenugreek seeds

100 ml rapeseed
or sunflower oil,
gently warmed

1 tbsp garam masala

½–1 tsp chilli powder

85 g dark brown sugar

Rub the limes with the salt. Cover and leave overnight at room temperature.

The next day, dry toast the cumin, fennel, mustard and fenugreek seeds in a frying pan. Allow to cool then grind.

Warm the oil gently in a saucepan, then stir in the ground spices, garam masala, chilli powder and sugar.

Allow to cool then mix with the limes.

Pack well into sterilized jars and leave to mature for two weeks.

The pickle keeps for up to six months. Once opened, it keeps for up to two weeks in the fridge.

Masala chai

Spice up your morning cup of tea with this much-loved Indian drink.

INGREDIENTS

2 mugs of milk (use nut or oat milk if you prefer)

½ cinnamon stick

6 cardamom pods, cracked

1 clove

1 star anise

1 cm fresh ginger, peeled and thinly sliced

2 tea bags (strong black tea is best)

2–4 tsp sugar

Heat the milk very gently and add the whole spices and tea bags.

Simmer for 5-10 minutes, depending on how strong you want it.

Strain and add sugar to taste.

N.B. If you don't like your tea too milky, dilute the milk with water.

Conclusion

As our whirlwind curry journey draws to a close, we have seen how this ancient approach to cooking has developed into a universally loved cuisine. The popularity of curry will seemingly never wane and it remains ever-evolving with the constant emergence of modern, vibrant recipes as tastes change and ingredients become more widely available.

There is a brief list of resources on the next page for some further insights into this mouth-watering topic, and the recipes in this book and elsewhere will hopefully inspire you to perfect the time-honoured art of making an amazing curry.

Of all cuisines, curry is perhaps the most open to experimentation, which makes it all the more exciting to explore. Approach your curry cooking as a fun adventure and you'll soon be producing sumptuous dishes to be proud of. Take pride in your creations and enjoy the smiles of your family and friends as they ask for more.

Resources

BOOKS

Anjum Anand, *Anjum's New Indian: Recipes from Indian Food Made Easy* (Quadrille, 2008)

Lizzy Collingham, *Curry: A Tale of Cooks and Conquerors* (Vintage, 2006)

Colleen Taylor Sen, *Curry: A Global History* (Speaking Tiger, 2017)

ARTICLES

Curry's Journey around the World

www.edition.cnn.com/travel/article/curry-origins-history/index.html

The Migration of Curries

www.fieryfoodscentral.com/2009/05/22/a-world-of-curries-north-india-and-pakistan/

The Origin of Mauritian Sept Cari

www.devas-kitchen.com/2016/01/16/the-mauritian-sept-cari-a-journey-of-tradition-and-adaptation/

THE LITTLE BOOK OF
CHILLIES

Rufus Cavendish

Paperback
ISBN: 978-1-80007-416-3

This book is a celebration of the all-conquering capsicum – from mild varieties to red-hot peppers – served with a spicy side of trivia, tips and recipes. The perfect pocket guide to these wonders of nature, it explores how they became so widely loved, where their heat comes from, and how they can beguile and benefit our bodies.

THE LITTLE BOOK OF
STUDENT FOOD

Alastair Williams

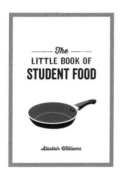

Paperback
ISBN: 978-1-78783-024-0

Every student needs to fill their belly as well as their brain. But even if you can barely make toast, this starter guide to killing it in the kitchen will give you what you need to succeed. From the very basics through to more adventurous dishes, these recipes are budget-friendly, super tasty and easy to make.

Have you enjoyed this book?
If so, find us on Facebook at
SUMMERSDALE PUBLISHERS, on Twitter at
@SUMMERSDALE and on Instagram at
@SUMMERSDALEBOOKS and get in touch.
We'd love to hear from you!

WWW.SUMMERSDALE.COM

IMAGE CREDITS